# STER⚾ID SPIRITUALITY

## HOW THE BIBLE CAN HELP US PLAY CLEAN

RHONDA JOY RUBINSON

# DEDICATION

*To those baseball players who play the game clean, whose feats on the baseball diamond we admire and enjoy, and whose conduct both on and off the field inspires us to be our best.*

# CONTENTS

# ACKNOWLEDGMENTS

I wish to gratefully acknowledge the contributions of New York Times sports writer William C. Rhoden and recently retired Baseball Commissioner Bud Selig. Bill's interview with me on the subject of spirituality and steroids for an article published by The Times led to a substantive phone conversation with Mr. Selig, which in turn inspired this small book. Thank you!

*Rhonda Joy Rubinson*
*December 24, 2014*

**Pregame Warm Up**

*How the Bible teaches us to play clean; Or, for a juice-less baseball future, consider Holy Scripture.*

Now that a peace treaty of sorts has been reached between Major League Baseball management and the Players Association in baseball's War on Steroids, it is time to consider how best to move into a healthier future. Like many fans, I would like to see a clean game, a fair playing field for all who compete at any level. As a member of society, I am especially interested in guiding our young people away from choices that might compromise their growth into healthy and productive adulthood. As a faith leader, I study the Bible daily, use it as a guide to my life, and teach others to do so. I propose that the Bible can provide guidance for both adults and young people on how to play clean, especially when

1

faced with the temptation to cheat.

Let me explain that last statement. I do not look to the Bible for specific answers to particular problems (*What should I have for lunch? Who should I marry? What house should I buy?*) but rather for general guiding principals (*How can I live the healthiest and most productive life? How can I turn a difficult situation into a positive one? What type of life will give me true and lasting satisfaction?*). These guiding principals can only be found when we read the Bible holistically, in order to identify the patterns of health and wholeness that permeate the entire book.

Sometimes it is not easy to read the Bible in this way. People want rules and answers, and while the Bible does provide some straightforward guidance, even seemingly clear guidelines can blur when examined closely. Take the Ten Commandments, for example. The injunction against working on the Sabbath raises further questions, such as: exactly what constitutes work? Several thousand years of debate have not entirely settled that question. Even the commandment "thou shalt not kill" was immediately understood by the new nation of Israel not as a blanket statement but rather to refer to unjustified killing (what we call murder) and not to killing in war, self-defense, and even in some cases, capital punishment. We can – and still do – argue the morality of taking a life in a multitude of different circumstances. But one fact that we can agree upon is that the Bible needs to be interpreted in order to apply it to a specific case.

The small book you are now reading aims to do just that, interpret biblical passages in order to apply them to a specific situation unknown in biblical times: steroid use in sports, specifically in baseball. I have drawn passages from both the Hebrew Scriptures and the New Testament, taking examples from the lives of biblical figures and using them to illuminate the stories of baseball players past and present to help us mold a better future. I offer these "nine innings" of biblical meditations to you, whether you are a young person or an adult, as an invitation to aspire to live the kind of life encouraged by the Bible, a life characterized by faith and integrity, rather than a life diminished, even squandered, by giving in to the temptation to cheat.

## 1<sup>st</sup> Inning

*Do what you are supposed to do, or you open the door to trouble.*

*And it came to pass, after the year was expired, at the time when kings go forth to battle, that David sent Joab, and his servants with him, and all Israel; and they destroyed the children of Ammon, and besieged Rabbah. But David tarried still at Jerusalem. And it came to pass in an eveningtide, that David arose from off his bed, and walked upon the roof of the king's house; and from the roof he saw a woman washing herself, and the woman was very beautiful to look upon. And David sent and enquired after the woman. And one said, is not this Bathsheba, the daughter of Eliam, the wife of Uriah the Hittite? And David sent messengers, and took her, and she came unto him, and he lay with her; for she was purified from her uncleanness: and she returned to her house. And the woman conceived and sent and told David, and said, I am with child.*
*– 2 Samuel 11:1-5 KJV*

During a normal American summer, owners finance

Major League baseball teams. Managers fill out lineup cards. Baseball players play. Umpires officiate. Fans fill the stands, cheer, and boo. Sports reporters blog, write, and talk. Vendors hawk. And so on.

In 1994, the baseball strike and the subsequent cancellation of the World Series disrupted this natural order, and the door was opened to trouble. Now we can argue the wisdom of the strike itself, which side bore ultimate responsibility for it, even whether there was a more or less moral side to the conflict. That is not our interest here, because it is irrelevant to what followed. The crux of the matter is that the strike stopped all who were even tangentially associated with Major League Baseball from doing what they normally do, and as a consequence we are still living with the troubles that entered the game – and our society – at that moment in time. The beginning of the ongoing moral crisis of the Steroid Era in baseball can be traced back to that lost season.

The Hebrew Scriptures have a story *par*

*excellence* that demonstrates the danger of not doing your job: the story of David and Bathsheba. At the time of year when it was the season for kings to go to battle, King David did not. The Second Book of Samuel does not tell us why – whether he was simply being lazy or whether he was ill or otherwise reasonably detained is not explained, again because it is irrelevant. The only pertinent fact is that King David was not doing what kings were supposed to do, and the temptations that await all of us when we don't fulfill our responsibilities were waiting for him. The Bible tells us that in the evening, David rose from his bed (evidently he had been resting all day), and went up to his roof where he saw the beautiful Bathsheba bathing.

What follows is disaster upon disaster: lust attacks David, he sends for the married Bathsheba, impregnates her, causes her innocent husband to be murdered in battle, loses the son born to Bathsheba as the offspring of the affair, and goes on to have a family that includes not only the famous Solomon but also a son who rapes his sister and is murdered by his brother in revenge. All because David tarried when it was the season for kings to go to battle.

When the baseball season was brought to a screeching halt in 1994, the consequences were likewise severe and generational, lasting to this present day. Even putting aside that many think that the 232-day strike had no clear winner, the damage was far-ranging: those in any way dependent on the sport lost money, and fans became convinced that neither side cared about them, even though it is the fans who are the founders of the MLB feast. The owners and the players chose to deadlock in a duel that could have resulted in the death of the professional game, and anger tinged with suspicion was born during the strike that persists as a corrosive cynicism towards the game to this day.

Worst of all, the desperation to save the game after it sustained such severe yet self-inflicted damage paved the way for widespread steroid use, which had begun in a localized way before the strike. And this in turn provided an irresistible incentive for owners, the Players Association, sports writers and even fans to look the other way when it came to "juiced" players. The obviously PED-fueled home run duel between Mark McGwire and Sammy Sosa in 1997 would not necessarily have been tolerated, let alone encouraged, if the fans had been treated to exciting, but normal, baseball in the summer of '94, a season which had plenty of compelling competitive stories to stoke interest. As a life-long Yankees fan, I was watching to see whether the Yanks and the aging Don Mattingly could reach the World Series. The Montreal Expos were likewise making an inspiring run for a Series berth. The wreckage of the shortened season and cancelled World Series created the climate of fear that permitted the poison of steroids to paralyze the nerves and distort the moral vision of otherwise decent and ethical people across all aspects of the game.

All because when it was the season for baseball players to battle, everyone tarried at home.

## 2<sup>nd</sup> Inning

**Eat your vegetables, no matter what anyone else says.**

*Daniel resolved that he would not defile himself with the royal rations of food and wine, so he asked the palace master to allow him not to defile himself. Now God allowed Daniel to receive favor and compassion from the palace master. The palace master said to Daniel, 'I am afraid of my lord the king; he has appointed your food and your drink. If he should see you in poorer condition than the other young men of your own age, you would endanger my head with the king.' Then Daniel asked the guard whom the palace master had appointed over Daniel, Hananiah, Mishael, and Azariah: 'Please test your servants for ten days. Let us be given vegetables to eat and water to drink. You can then compare our appearance with the appearance of the young men who eat the royal rations, and deal with your servants according to what you observe.' So he agreed to this proposal and tested them for ten days. At the end of ten days it was observed that they appeared better and fatter than all the young men who had been eating the royal rations. So the guard continued to withdraw their royal rations and the wine they were to drink, and gave them vegetables. To these four young men God gave knowledge and skill in every aspect of literature and wisdom; Daniel also had insight into all visions and dreams. - Daniel 1:7-16*

No one needs to take steroids, ever.

It is hard to imagine greater pressure to corrupt one's body than the pressure that was brought to bear on Daniel and his three companions in the court of the Babylonian king Nebuchadnezzar. The four young Jewish men had already endured much: members of the noble class under King Jehoiakim in the early 7th century BC, they were captured by the Babylonians and taken to the king's palace to be trained as court advisors. Already Jewish captives in a strange land, Daniel and his friends were forced to train in pagan philosophy. If that weren't pressure enough for them to compromise their Jewish principles to please their captors, they were also given the palace food and drink, which were obviously not in accord with what the young Jewish men were used to eating according to the Law (the main danger appears to have been accidentally eating food – especially meat – that was sacrificed to Babylonian idols).

In refusing the king's food, the young men put more than their own lives in danger – the palace master in charge of feeding the young men could have faced lethal punishment for disobeying the king's personal order to feed the newest court members the palace fare of rich food and wine. But Daniel would not budge. Displaying the cleverness and courage that later become features of his behavior in such situations, Daniel suggests a test: feed the four of us with water and vegetables for ten days, proposes Daniel, then judge the results. The palace master agrees, and the outcome is startling. Daniel and his three friends are found to be stronger, healthier, even fatter than those who ate the royal food.

The God of Israel has obviously intervened at

this point. Today we know through science what those in Daniel's time knew by experience and intuition: the king's food and wine were much higher in fat and calories than vegetables and water, yet the young men were rewarded by God not only with better general health (which might be expected from a vegetarian diet, although I'm not advocating that here) but they were found to be even heavier than their pagan counterparts. To drive the message home, the Bible adds that "God gave knowledge and skill in every aspect of literature and wisdom" to the four young men. Furthermore, Daniel, their leader, was shown special favor by God, who gifted him with "insight into all visions and dreams." All because they stayed faithful to God by eating their vegetables

Temptations to go against what one knows to be right, especially pertaining to what we ingest in our bodies, are as potent today as they were in Daniel's time. How many of us can resist an advertisement for fast food if we're hungry, let alone stand up to a threat to our lives if we refuse savory royal food? I know I cave in to temptation every time I pass a McDonald's on a road trip; Lord knows what I would do if I was offered tasty food along with a threat if I didn't eat it.

Furthermore, how many of us who have an addiction to drugs or alcohol could be strong enough to refuse those substances when they are being passed around, and everyone is partaking of them? Alcoholics and addicts know that hard as it is to stay sober and straight, it is much harder when the trouble is not only available, but peer pressure to join the party comes to bear as well. These temptations are not limited to feeling pleasantly high or powerful physically: the lures of success, big money, fame, and fan adulation can be as powerful as any drug. Add the competitive fire of any true athlete, impatience to recover from injuries, and the physical pressure of a long baseball season, and it is easy to see why PEDs are so enticing.

But even a quick glance at the consequences

suffered by juicers should cause every potential user to pause. Rewards can slip out of the grasp of those who use drugs in pursuit of wealth, fame, and adulation. Even players of incandescent talent who have been suspected of PED use but not caught – like Barry Bonds and Roger Clemens – are finding their legacies greatly diminished and the possibility of their being elected to the Baseball Hall of Fame fast vanishing. The then-thrilling home run chase by Mark McGwire and Sammy Sosa is now viewed by fans more like a WWE championship match than a serious baseball contest for the ages: fun while it lasted, but not real enough to respect. The long-term value of such careers and records will forever be suspect, and will always be judged "less-than" the records that have stood the test of time from the pre-steroid era.

If those consequences aren't bad enough, the long-term effects on one's body from steroid use are even worse, and can be life-threatening. Heart problems, sexual dysfunction, and mental health issues like violent behavior, anxiety, anger, depression and even suicidal thoughts and actions, can all torment the user. Lives can – and have been – forever altered, even destroyed, because of juicing.

The lesson of Daniel is clear: eat God's vegetables, not the world's meat. Don't consume everything served up to you by the culture surrounding you. God can always find a way to supply the missing calories

*3rd Inning*

***Everything must be done in the correct order;***
***steps cannot be reversed or skipped.***

*Moses set up the tabernacle; he laid its bases, and
set up its frames, and put in its poles, and raised up
its pillars; and he spread the tent over the
tabernacle, and put the covering of the tent over it;
as the LORD had commanded Moses. He took the
covenant and put it into the ark, and put the poles
on the ark, and set the mercy-seat above the
ark; and he brought the ark into the tabernacle, and
set up the curtain for screening, and screened the
Ark of the Covenant; as the LORD had commanded
Moses. He put the table in the tent of meeting, on
the north side of the tabernacle, outside the
curtain, and set the bread in order on it before
the LORD; as the LORD had commanded Moses. He
put the lampstand in the tent of meeting, opposite
the table on the south side of the tabernacle, and set
up the lamps before the LORD; as the LORD had
commanded Moses. He put the golden altar in the
tent of meeting before the curtain, and offered
fragrant incense on it; as the LORD had commanded*

17

*Moses. He also put in place the screen for the entrance of the tabernacle. He set the altar of burnt-offering at the entrance of the tabernacle of the tent of meeting, and offered on it the burnt-offering and the grain-offering as the LORD had commanded Moses. He set the basin between the tent of meeting and the altar, and put water in it for washing, with which Moses and Aaron and his sons washed their hands and their feet. When they went into the tent of meeting, and when they approached the altar, they washed; as the LORD had commanded Moses. He set up the court around the tabernacle and the altar, and put up the screen at the gate of the court. So Moses finished the work. – Exodus 40:18-33*

Every baseball player knows that you stretch before you run, you soft toss before you air out a fastball, you loosen up before you swing a bat as hard as you can. Skipping steps or doing things in the wrong order invites disaster. Similarly, if you want to create anything – a delicious meal, a beautiful painting, a tabernacle (a tent to hold the presence of God), or even a baseball player at the top of his game – you have to do things in order. Steps cannot be skipped or reversed, or the whole project can be ruined.

This is a more profound concept than it seems at first glance, with penalties if we try to circumvent it that are far more serious than being placed on the DL with a torn muscle. For believers in the Bible, the act of creation is sacred: it is the primary way that we reflect the glory of our Creator, the author of creation, in whose image we are made. Acts of creation are what set us apart from the rest of the animal kingdom. Although other life forms may use language, make tools, even work together towards a common end, we are the only creatures who are capable of creating solely for the sake of creating, who take special care to craft something especially beautiful, delicious, or meaningful for ourselves, our families, our communities, and our God.

The pursuit of athletic excellence falls into this category of uniquely human creation. A skilled, trained athlete is a wonder to behold, a sublime creation who at his or her peak does honor to God. A team of such athletes of disparate skills but common effort working towards a shared purpose can result in a championship team, another way of honoring God.

In the passage from Exodus above, Moses takes special care to do exactly what God has told him to do in exactly the order in which he was instructed in the most excellent way possible. For Moses this is a form of worship. To make sure no one misses the model that Moses is emulating while building God's tabernacle, the author constructs the narrative as a parallel to the creation story in Genesis. Just as the seven days of creation build upon each other, the creation of the tabernacle is carefully ordered, too. As each step of creation was finished with the phrase "and it was evening and it was morning," each step in the building of the tabernacle is divided from the next by the phrase "as the Lord commanded Moses." And yes, there are seven steps as Moses creates God's tabernacle, as there are seven steps ("days") in God's creation of the universe.

Here we learn that God expects two things

from his faithful children. The first is that we would do well to pray for God's guidance for whatever we undertake. We can expect that the instructions we receive in response to our prayers are not going to be as specific as the plans that God gave to Moses for the tabernacle, but we can and should always abide by a clear rule given to us for health and ultimate success: don't put poison in your body. Although steroids may give you a temporary advantage in muscle mass and quick reflexes, eventually your body will break down, and your career will be tainted.

The second lesson is that things must be done in the correct order, or the whole enterprise may fall apart. Moses had to lay the base and the frame first, then install the poles and the pillars. If he had tried to install the poles first, he would not have been able to spread the tent that would protect the sacred ark, and not incidentally keep it from public view.

There is a third deep lesson here too, and that is that certain precious things must be hidden, that they will be ruined or even do harm if they are exposed too soon. Glory that is revealed to the world is always accompanied by what cannot be seen: mountains have roots far deeper than what we see above the earth or sea. Likewise, athletes cannot expect to have lasting glory without following the God-given laws of nature: consistent effort and training hidden from the public eye, development of skills in the correct order with no skipping of steps, all done with submission to God's laws of health and salvation.

No steroids.

**4<sup>th</sup> Inning**

*Always listen to the still, small voice in your spirit,
not to the loudest voices around you.*

*The Lord said (to Elijah), 'Go out and stand on the
mountain before the Lord, for the Lord is about to
pass by.' Now there was a great wind, so strong
that it was splitting mountains and breaking rocks
in pieces before the Lord, but the Lord was not in
the wind; and after the wind an earthquake, but the
Lord was not in the earthquake; and after the
earthquake a fire, but the Lord was not in the fire;
and after the fire a sound of sheer silence. – 1 Kings
19:11-12*

The song says that we go looking for love in all the
wrong places. We also go looking for God in all the
wrong places.

We think that because God is so much bigger
than us, so much greater than us, so much more

powerful than us that this incomprehensibly enormous God must appear to us accompanied by cataclysmic noise and terror. Yet in the Bible, when mortals meet God, it is almost always in the context of *a conversation*. Although there might be a spectacular phenomenon or two to get someone's attention (think: Moses and the burning bush, or Paul and the blinding burst of light on the Road to Damascus), the actual encounter involves a message. God doesn't just wow people or seek to shock them into submission; rather, God wants to talk to his children, and become partners with them.

In the passage from the First Book of Kings above, Elijah has been hiding out in a cave because Queen Jezebel was out to kill him. This most famous and powerful of prophets had just defeated five hundred priests of Baal in spectacular fashion, and the queen was embarrassed and infuriated. Elijah runs away as far and as fast as he can, but it is no surprise that God finds him where he thinks he cannot be found, hiding in a cave. After Elijah tells him that he is running for his life to escape Jezebel, the Lord decides to show him a thing or two about what to truly fear, and not incidentally where to truly find God.

God's demonstration consists of three terrifying natural phenomena (which just happen to be ones that we curiously call "Acts of God" in our insurance policies). The first is a cataclysmic wind, like a tornado; the second is a violent earthquake; the third is a massive wildfire, of the sort that can be started by lightning in dry brush. Like much imagery in the Bible, these natural phenomena can be considered on a symbolic level in addition to the physical: the wind stands in for of the voices of temptation, harassment, or peer pressure; the earthquake is symbolic of the "shaking out" or destruction of our material possessions, including money; and the fire represents pain and suffering, whether physical, mental, or spiritual. The Bible makes it clear that God is not *in* any of these natural disasters. This does not mean that God does not allow them to happen, however; we'll get to why in a minute.

For now, we are learning the first lesson God is teaching Elijah: that the voice of God is not to be found in the noise of disaster. Rather, God is found in the "sound of sheer silence," sometimes translated as the "still, small voice." A true encounter with God, while certainly overwhelming, is not terrifying in the sense of cataclysm but rather awe-inspiring. Most important of all, a true message from God is what we hear when all else is silenced, when we listen to the "voice" deep in our spirit. We usually don't hear this "voice" in spoken words (although some people do); the most common description of "God's voice" is that it is a strong impression, a deep knowing, a definite sense that we are receiving a communication from outside of ourselves that is powerful, sure, and above all, loving.

This "voice" often leads us in a direction that contradicts our own desires or fears. When Elijah finally quiets down enough to listen, God doesn't even mention the dreaded Jezebel. Instead God gives Elijah instructions on who to anoint as the next king of Israel, and who to anoint as Elijah's own successor. The perceived danger that so terrified Elijah is not a problem at all, but he had to hear the true voice of God, deep in the "sound of sheer silence," in order to discern *God's* concerns and forget about his own.

These days, our lives are so filled with noise and distraction that sometimes God will allow a crisis to confront us in order to get our attention, to encourage us to seek him. But if we form a habit of listening to God, God won't have to "wake us up." Any athlete considering using steroids can consciously detach himself from the voices that say "go ahead, it'll give you an edge, it's the only way you can be a champion, think of the fame, think of the money, imagine the adulation" and sit quietly to listen for the still, small voice of God. When the answer is "no matter how much you want to, don't go there," then there is a choice. You can obey the voice of God, or you can go your own way and give in to the pressure around you, the voice that does not belong to God.

However, here's a "heads-up" for those who choose to follow God. Be aware that *if you do the right thing, you can expect a backlash, because the decision to follow God instead of the world will not be without cost.* Although we have reached a point in time when the culture of Major League Baseball is finally shifting, turning against steroid use with more rigorous testing and tougher penalties now in place, that doesn't mean that those who refuse to cheat won't be shunned in some way. It also doesn't mean that the temptation to take steroids or some newer, as yet undetectable designer drug won't come along. The pressure to cheat to find an edge will always be present in some form.

But if you keep faithful to God's wishes for your best life, you will eventually be rewarded. Sandy Koufax, who was Jewish, stuck to his observance of the Sabbath even during the World Series, despite strong opposition. It could be argued that he of all people could do that because he was, after all, Sandy Koufax – but the reverse could be argued as well:  that his success as a all-time great was a reward from God for observing the Sabbath for many years before ever throwing a Major League pitch.  God knows how to reward us in public for the sacrifices we make when we obey him in private.

The lesson:  Choose the voices that you allow to influence you very carefully.  Listen for the voice of God, and God will guide you along the right path.

*5<sup>th</sup> Inning*

***Perhaps, like Queen Esther, you were born for such a time as this; Or there's more than one way to be a hero.***

*Hathach went out to Mordecai in the open square of the city in front of the king's gate, and Mordecai told him all that had happened to him, and the exact sum of money that Haman had promised to pay into the king's treasuries for the destruction of the Jews. Mordecai also gave him a copy of the written decree issued in Susa for their destruction, that he might show it to Esther, explain it to her, and charge her to go to the king to make supplication to him and entreat him for her people. Hathach went and told Esther what Mordecai had said. Then Esther spoke to Hathach and gave him a message for Mordecai, saying, 'All the king's servants and the people of the king's provinces know that if any man or woman goes to the king inside the inner court without being called, there is but one law—all alike are to be put to death. Only if the king holds out the golden scepter to someone, may that person live. I myself have not been called to come in to the king for thirty days.' When they told Mordecai what Esther had said, Mordecai told them to reply to Esther, 'Do not think that in the king's palace you will escape any more than all the other Jews. For if you keep silence at such a time as this, relief and deliverance will rise for the Jews from another quarter, but you and your father's family will perish. Who knows? Perhaps you have come to royal dignity for just such a time as this.' – Esther 4:6-14*

Who knows why we have been put on earth at this specific time and place, in our particular set of circumstances? God certainly knows the answer to that question for each of us, but we often don't have a clue as to our purpose until we look back on the events of our lives in hindsight; only then do we realize that we have played a role in God's plan that had remained hidden from us at the time.

It's therefore not surprising that the question "why were we born?" haunts many of us who do not yet know our true purpose. Why? Because we think our purpose is our responsibility, when in fact it is God's decision. We love to think that we are in control, that we design our own lives and carve out our own destiny. This is partly true – God created us to be his partners, not his puppets. But as the 19th century British priest Jeremy Taylor says in his classic book *Holy Living*, our job is not to author the play (or the plan of the world), but to play our part well. But that begs the question: how can we know *what* role God wants us to play?

The scientist Louis Pasteur once famously said, "Chance favors only the prepared mind." By this he meant at least two things: that that you must work hard in your field to be prepared to make an important contribution when the opportunity arises, and that your imagination must be open to possibilities that have previously been inconceivable. Ignore either preparation or imagination and the chance of a lifetime to make your mark may fly by unrecognized, or, you won't be prepared to take advantage of it even if you perceive the opportunity for what it is.

Each of us is dealt a hand to play when we are

born. The circumstances of our birth are partly environmental (where we are born, our family situation, the availability of basic necessities in our community, and so on), and partly genetic (natural gifts and talents, genetic predispositions for both achievement and illness). But these circumstances are no more than starting points – they are in no way a guarantee of where we will finish. That is up to us. Faith and discipline are much more indicative of our future success than any natural or environmental advantage or disadvantage we may have received at birth.

A ball player is human, like all of us. He has no idea how God will ultimately use him, but he may very well leave a legacy that surpasses winning an MVP or Cy Young award. We'll get to the story of pitcher Armando Gallaraga's "imperfect perfect game" in a moment; first let's look at the question of destiny and what the Bible teaches us about how to prepare for our destiny. Hint: in baseball the preparation has nothing to do with cheating.

The biblical Queen Esther is an excellent

example of how to prepare yourself to play the role that God has chosen for you once you have stepped into your destiny. Esther was born into a Jewish family whose forebears had been taken into exile during the Babylonian captivity of Judah. She was orphaned at an early age, then adopted by her uncle Mordecai, a respected member of the Jewish community who were generally despised and regularly persecuted first by their Babylonian captors, then by the Persians who conquered Babylon. Obviously, this was not the most advantageous start in life for Esther, but she advanced from a persecuted female orphan to Queen of Persia and God's chosen means of salvation for the Jewish people. All because she was prepared.

Despite the circumstantial challenges of her birth, Esther had two things going for her: she was beautiful, and she was obedient. As she grew into womanhood, it never occurred to her to dream of a position in the King of Persia's palace; in fact the very thought would have been repugnant to her as a

Jew. Yet when the king banished (and possibly killed) his favorite wife, Queen Vashti, for insubordination, it was Esther of all the maidens in the vast kingdom who the king chose to replace her. Esther's only preparation was spiritual: she had habitually submitted herself to Mordecai, and she learned from him to submit herself to God, and also to the pagan authorities.

Mordecai had set a powerful example for her when heard of a plot to assassinate the king and reported it to the palace. When the plot was stopped, Mordecai was recorded as having been loyal to the king, despite being a Jew. So Esther had no problem obeying the king while remaining faithful to God when she herself reached the palace.

When God elevated her to a position that she had not sought or desired, she proved crucial to God's salvation of Israel. When the wicked Haman, the king's second in command, plotted to destroy the Jewish people because Mordecai wouldn't bow to him, Mordecai sent word to Esther of the plot and reminded her that God had placed her in a position that could save the Jewish people, but that she must be faithful and courageous, or she would forfeit the unparalleled opportunity that had been given her.

This was no easy matter – there was considerable personal danger, since the king could order Esther put to death for her disobedience. If she were selfish, Esther could easily have been tempted to think only of herself, since she was now safely ensconced in the palace as the king's favorite. Yet despite the risks, Esther hearkened to Mordecai when he said, *'if you keep silence at such a time as this, relief and deliverance will rise for the Jews from another quarter, but you and your father's family will perish. Who knows? Perhaps you have come to royal dignity for just such a time as this.'*

The outcome of the story is well known: Esther succeeds in reversing the decree of genocide meant for the Jewish people, and the evil Haman is hanged on the gallows he had prepared for Mordecai. For our purpose, the point is this: Esther had prepared for her moment of destiny by training herself to be faithful, and by keeping her mind open to possibilities she never imagined, both in becoming queen and by become God's chosen instrument of salvation.

There is a recent, highly unusual example of this kind of unplanned heroism, this time on the baseball field. On June 2, 2010, Tigers pitcher Armando Gallaraga was within one out of throwing a perfect game against the Indians. (As you probably know, perfect games are a rarity, a feat that only twenty pitchers to that date had accomplished.) When Indians shortstop Jason Donald softly grounded to first baseman Miguel Cabrera and Cabrera tossed to Gallaraga covering first, almost everyone on the field and in the stands thought that Gallaraga had his perfect game.

The one exception was first base umpire Jim Joyce, who called Donald safe. Joyce had blown the call, but that is when the opportunity arose for both Gallaraga and Joyce to really shine. Everyone expected Gallaraga to be furious, to claim that he was robbed of his rightful achievement, maybe even to protest the call and the game to the MLB front office. Similarly, everyone expected Joyce to stand his ground, since umpires are not known for admitting mistakes or for apologizing.

Instead, what happened next reverberated far outside the lines on the diamond. Gallaraga immediately forgave Joyce, saying after the game "Nobody's perfect." Then Joyce admitted he blew the call, emotionally apologized to Gallaraga personally, and then did the same in public, in front of the media. The two men even greeted each other with a hug before the game the following day, and there was an outpouring of support from players, fans, even government officials, for both men.

This was called "sportsmanship" in the papers, but the lessons go far beyond a simple display of sportsmanship, valuable as that is. On June 2, 2010, Gallaraga and Joyce thought they had showed up at Comerica Park to participate in a baseball game. Neither man had expected to be in a position to have a positive effect on society by setting powerful examples of forgiveness, repentance, and compassion through their actions. Yet that is exactly what happened, and the day turned out to be far more memorable than even had Gallaraga pitched a historic perfect game. Instead, that game was a true "Esther moment," one that showed that both men had carefully prepared their characters in addition to their baseball skills before stepping on the field. As a result, they have attained lasting fame that they had not sought when circumstances provided an unusual opportunity for transcending the game. Not only did he not cheat, Gallaraga did not even push for what was rightfully his according to the rules. And Joyce did not dig in his heels and play the pre-programmed role of the infallible umpire. Instead, both men rose to the occasion when God offered them a moment of transformative dignity beyond what they could have imagined.

Who knows if they had been born for such a time as this? Who knows what time *you* were born for? Prepare both your skills and your character, and you might be rewarded with the chance to have an effect on the world far beyond the diamond.

## 6<sup>th</sup> Inning

**Do it God's way, you'll be much more successful than if you follow your own impulses.**

*Jesus showed himself again to the disciples by the Sea of Tiberias; and he showed himself in this way. Gathered there together were Simon Peter, Thomas called the Twin, Nathanael of Cana in Galilee, the sons of Zebedee, and two others of his disciples. Simon Peter said to them, 'I am going fishing.' They said to him, 'We will go with you.' They went out and got into the boat, but that night they caught nothing. Just after daybreak, Jesus stood on the beach; but the disciples did not know that it was Jesus. Jesus said to them, 'Children, you have no fish, have you?' They answered him, 'No.' He said to them, 'Cast the net to the right side of the boat, and you will find some.' So they cast it, and now they were not able to haul it in because there were so many fish. That disciple whom Jesus loved said to Peter, 'It is the Lord!' When Simon Peter heard that it was the Lord, he put on some*

*clothes, for he was naked, and jumped into the lake.*
*– John 21:1-7*


Our feelings, even our past training, are not always reliable guides on how to pursue future success. This is particularly true once we have outgrown a stage in our lives, as we are moving into a new level of experience, maturity, and knowledge. Athletic training is an important part of success in sports, but we need to train our characters and spirits in addition to our bodies. In any case, what worked for us in the past might need to change in the present for success in the future.

The reading above from the Gospel of John is an object lesson on how to be led by God to change our approach, no matter how successful we've been. Simon Peter had worked for many years as a professional fisherman, as had some of his fellow apostles before they heeded the call to follow Jesus. But that was in their past, this is now their present, in the time following Jesus' crucifixion. Finding himself in the position of attempting to reconstruct his life after what seemed to be the unmitigated disaster of Jesus' death, Peter did what many of us would do in his place: return to the work he had done before he met Jesus. Remember that these fishermen did not lose their fishing skills while they were following Jesus; they still knew where to look for fish, what time of the day was best for a haul, in what conditions, and so forth. Yet all of their knowledge did not produce the expected result: they fished all night long, yet caught nothing. We are reminded of the disclaimer that appears in every advertisement for corporate stock: "Past performance is no guarantee of future returns."

This often happens to us in our own lives. What has worked for us before has stopped working, no matter how reliable our methods used to be. This is particularly true once we have had an intimate experience with God. Peter and his fellow apostles were transformed by their journey with Jesus, and although they think that the discipleship phase of their lives has ended, they find that they cannot simply pick up where they left off. What used to be easy for them is now hard; the methods that they formerly counted on now reap nothing but disappointment.

That is, until Jesus arrives on the scene. As is usually the case after his resurrection, Jesus is not immediately recognizable, even to those with whom he was close. Part of this is lack of expectation: the apostles know that Jesus is dead and buried, so they certainly don't expect to see him walking around. In addition, Jesus was the son of a carpenter, not a fisherman, yet this stranger seems to know more about fishing than they do. Furthermore, the stranger tells them to push the boat back out to sea and fish some more when they are exhausted from toiling unsuccessfully all night long. And to top it all off, he tells them to cast the net off what they know to be the wrong side of the boat!

But – because Peter was willing to do what he didn't want to do when he didn't think it would work, *because he trusted in an authority outside of himself* – he was rewarded with astounding success, a haul of fish so big that it threatened to break the net and sink the boat.

Never underestimate the power of trying new things. Be open to influences other than your own will. Of course, always work hard. But find coaches and mentors and role models who you respect and admire to give you guidance outside of the familiar. Pray. Listen. Trust God, even when God points you in a direction different than the one you would choose for yourself. Know that time passes, recognize that you are in a different place now; you are a wiser person, so your methods can change, too. As you mature, allow God to lead you more and more. Success can be as simple as casting the net off of the other side of the boat, even when you think it won't work. Learn from Peter, and see what kind of harvest God will give you.

## 7<sup>th</sup> Inning

### Adulation is fleeting: remember Palm Sunday

*The disciples went and did as Jesus had directed them; they brought the donkey and the colt, and put their cloaks on them, and he sat on them. A very large crowd spread their cloaks on the road, and others cut branches from the trees and spread them on the road. The crowds that went ahead of him and that followed were shouting, 'Hosanna to the Son of David! Blessed is the one who comes in the name of the Lord! Hosanna in the highest heaven!' When he entered Jerusalem, the whole city was in turmoil, asking, 'Who is this?' – Matthew 21:6-10*

Do you remember the advertising campaign featuring tennis great Andre Agassi whose catchphrase was, "Image is everything"?

That famous slogan by camera manufacturer Canon was meant as a double entendre:    the

46

company was both touting the high quality of their digital cameras (no argument there, I've owned Canons and they indeed produce great images), and promoting the use of their cameras for people to construct an "image" that will win them fame and fortune. Those 1990's ads both hooked into and helped energize the huge, world-wide increase in narcissism and undeserved fame that we are still living with today (watch any reality television program if you have any doubt as to how far we have sunk into the morass that begins with believing that "image is everything").

Well, that ad campaign is a myth: far from being everything, "image" is actually close to nothing. "Image" is insubstantial and ephemeral, subject to capricious fads and the fickle nature of those bestowing the image with importance. Those showered with fame and adulation today can be the object of hostility, ridicule, and scandal tomorrow.

That's what happened to Jesus – adulation morphed into anger against him – and he did not sin to provoke the change in attitude. He didn't have to. The whims of the masses needed nothing more than a rumor to provoke a complete about-face from adulation to hatred. The crowds accompanying Jesus on his triumphant entry into Jerusalem who were shouting "Hosanna to the Son of David! Blessed is he who comes in the name of the Lord!" are the same people who cried, "Crucify him!" just a few days later. These same folks heard Jesus preach parables about the kingdom of God, ate of miraculous bread at the feeding of the five thousand, saw people healed at Jesus' hands, even knew that he had resurrected a dead man, Lazarus. But when some priests and elders accuse Jesus of blasphemy, the base human desire to see the acclaimed brought down took over. We see this play out in our own day, as respected and admired public figures frequently topple in our world.

If that was what happened to Jesus, what will happen to those of us who have attempted to cover up actual wrongdoing? We don't have to look very far; the examples are before us every day in the media. There are a particularly large number of fallen heroes in baseball: Mark McGwire, Sammy Sosa, Rafael Palmiero, Ryan Braun and Alex Rodriguez, just to name a few of the A-list players who have chosen to enmesh themselves in the steroid culture. A few scant years ago all of these men were national heroes, fêted and handsomely compensated for their record-setting achievements on the baseball field. Where are they all now? Except for Braun and Rodriguez, who have been undeniably tarnished, but whose character and behavior continue to be dissected since they are still currently active, the rest have been disgraced. Most are now pariahs in the game to which they devoted their lives.

The possible exception is McGwire, who is arguably the least compromised personally, since the substance he used during his chase of Roger Maris' home run record wasn't banned by the MLB at the time he used it, although is was banned by other major sports as a known steroid; the rest knowingly used banned drugs. McGwire was hired as the hitting coach for the St. Louis Cardinals in

2009, and by the LA Dodgers in 2013. But he is not in the Hall of Fame, and likely never will be. His single season home run record has a bigger asterisk next to it in the record book than Maris' ever did. And he will be forever remembered for his cringe-worthy testimony in front of the House Government Reform Committee where he robotically parroted a canned response to repeated questions about his personal steroid use ("I'm not here to talk about the past . . .").

How quickly it all changed for them. Is the fleeting taste of adulation and wealth worth the consequences? Remember, when all the crowds turn and leave, when the image falls apart, you are left with living with yourself, and with facing God. It may be a tougher road to travel, and the rewards may come more slowly, but the peace of God and a clear conscience are permanent rewards that no one can ever take from you.

## 8<sup>th</sup> Inning

### Don't think you can get away with it.

*Meanwhile, when the crowd gathered in thousands, so that they trampled on one another, Jesus began to speak first to his disciples, 'Beware of the yeast of the Pharisees, that is, their hypocrisy. Nothing is covered up that will not be uncovered, and nothing secret that will not become known. Therefore whatever you have said in the dark will be heard in the light, and what you have whispered behind closed doors will be proclaimed from the housetops. I tell you, my friends, do not fear those who kill the body, and after that can do nothing more. But I will warn you whom to fear: fear him who, after he has killed, has authority to cast into hell. Yes, I tell you, fear him!' – Luke 12:1-5*

*For God will bring every deed into judgment, including every secret thing, whether good or evil. – Ecclesiastes 11:13*

How tempting it is to believe that no one will ever discover when we cheat. Countless careers – and lives – have been ruined throughout history by those who thought that they were special, somehow exempt from the rules that govern everyone else, that they alone could get away with bad, illegal, sinful behavior and receive all good results and no adverse consequences. It may happen in the next few hours, weeks, or days; it may take years; or the bad behavior may "die with you," but even then "nothing is covered up that will not be uncovered, and nothing (is) secret that will not become known."

Can we ever truly believe that no one knows when we cheat? The hard truth is that we can never cheat on our own; we always need the help of others. And the people we think will never rat on us or testify against us if caught will always do so when their own life is on the line. Consider the line-up of suppliers, trainers, even teammates who have turned against the players that they helped juice; these are people that were entrusted with a dark secret, who sometimes signed confidentiality agreements, and who are now the lead witnesses for the prosecution. Do you really want to entrust your body and your reputation to men like Anthony Bosch or Brian McNamee? How can anyone believe that people who cheat themselves will keep their word to those whom they help to cheat?

Beneath these questions lie deeper ones, questions so basic that they may surprise you. The first deep, basic question is this: why do you play baseball? Or if you are a professional ballplayer – why do you continue to play baseball as an adult? It is easy to see why children and young people play baseball – it's fun, it's challenging, and we can all learn lessons on the field that can carry us far in life, like how to be part of a team, how hard work produces results, and how to handle both success and failure. But when an adult man steps on to a baseball diamond, the answers to that question have necessarily changed. Yes, the game can and should continue to be fun at the professional level, but now there is money involved, possibly big money along with fame, which are lures that a child does not face. Inevitably – and admirably – the desire to reach the highest level of the game in the MLB comes into play, along with the recognition of skill and talent that attaining that exalted level confers. There is the awareness that potentially millions of people will watch every move on the field, whether good or bad. Finally, an adult ball player is painfully aware that the clock is ticking on his career, so the understandable tendency is to try to collect the most wealth in the relatively short window of time that he will have as an active player.

As the temptation to cheat grows with all of those complicating temptations and pressures, we can forget that sooner or later we will be found out if we do. So the question still remains: why are you playing baseball as an adult? It helps to revisit this question often, to do a "heart check-up," so to speak. Asking this question will help identify changing reasons for sticking with the game, and perhaps catch the slide into dangerous behavior.

A second deep, basic question is this: are we aware that we are always in God's presence, that God understands all our desires, knows all of our thoughts, sees all of our actions? In essence, that is what Jesus is telling us in the reading above when he says, "what you have said in the dark will be heard in the light." And the author of Ecclesiastes is even more blunt: every deed will be judged, even if it was done in secret, for good or for evil.

The Bible shows us repeatedly that we cannot flee from God, no matter how hard we try. Adam and Eve try to hide from God in the Garden of Eden, to no avail. Jonah the prophet tries to flee from God in a boat, and he winds up in the belly of a huge fish. In Psalm 139, the psalmist says: "Where can I go from your spirit? Or where can I flee from your presence? If I ascend to heaven, you are there; if I make my bed in Sheol (the underworld), you are there. If I take the wings of the morning and settle at the farthest limits of the sea, even there your hand shall lead me, and your right hand shall hold me fast."

No one can ever escape God's presence. Just because we turn our attention away from God does not mean that God's attention is turned away from us. But the good news is that when we try to flee from God, God will seek us out to bring us back, pricking our conscience, keeping us up at night with the nagging feeling that all is not well. Often, when we say, "our conscience is bothering us," what we really mean is that God is telling us that we have strayed from the right path, and that repentance is necessary.

The good news is that God loves us no matter what we have done, and that God is always ready to forgive us. But are we ready to be forgiven? Just look at the last line of Psalm 139 quoted above: "If I take the wings of the morning and settle at the farthest limits of the sea, even there your hand shall lead me, and your right hand shall hold me fast." No matter how far we've strayed, God is always right next to us, ready to take our hand, to love us, forgive us, and strengthen us to do his will. God will always help us to live our lives in the right way, even after we've done wrong.

Are you hiding something in the dark? If so, are you ready for it to be revealed in the light? Because that time will surely come. If you've strayed, return to the right path. Repent and ask God to help you not to cheat again. God is waiting with open arms to welcome you back.

## 9th Inning

### Aspire to be the best you can be; Or, God's economy is different than the world's economy.

*For to those who have, more will be given, and they will have an abundance; but from those who have nothing, even what they have will be taken away. – Matthew 13:12*

In our world's economy, gain is the result of our own efforts. Often, we attain wealth at the expense of others. There are sayings that we use to describe the way the world's economy works: "More for me, less for you," "You need money to make money," "I need to look out for number one," are just a few.

Did you know that God has an economy too? But God's economy of grace does not work the way the world's economy does. In God's economy, there is more than enough for everyone; God's abundance is endless. You become wealthy by giving away what you have. You don't need wealth to make more wealth; you need faith in God's grace. And you certainly don't need to look out for yourself in any kind of selfish way; in fact we are encouraged to be as generous as possible with all of the gifts God has given us, material and spiritual. Finally, we are told repeatedly that if we live our lives with God at the center rather than ourselves, God promises to look out for us. And God is always faithful to his promises.

The Bible verse above from the Gospel of Matthew seems to be a paradox. Why would God give to those who already have? How can God "take away" from those who have nothing? The answer is that Jesus is only *partly* talking about money. Mostly what he is talking about is wealth of faith and spiritual character. "Those who have" are those who believe in God, obeying the commandments to "Love the Lord your God with all your heart, soul, mind and strength, and love your neighbor as yourself." As a result, "those who have" gain more wealth in God's economy, and they will often be rewarded in ways visible to the world. "Those who have nothing" are those who have been proud and selfish, who don't care for the wealth of God's economy. Their gains are ill gotten; as a consequence they have a low balance in God's economy. From those people, even what they think they have gained will be confiscated from them. Some things that can be removed from "those who have nothing" are monetary wealth, baseball records, and reputation, not to mention peace of mind.

Fortunately, there are plenty of examples of "those who have" in baseball history, those who earned wealth in God's eyes and who became famous for both their athletic prowess and character. Take, for example, the first players to break racial and ethnic barriers. They insured themselves legacies far beyond the ball field by playing the game at the Major League level despite the virulent prejudice often directed at them not only by fans but also by their own teammates and baseball management. Because of the barriers that they faced, the first ball players of an oppressed group needed to be more talented and more courageous than white players of the same era in order first to make it to the bigs, and then to remain there. Jackie Robinson had to be – and certainly was – a prodigious talent of strong character and courage in order to be the African American who broke the Major League color barrier. His contributions not only to baseball, but to the nation outside of baseball (he also broke barriers in business and banking after his retirement from the field) will always stand as a shining example of what every American should aspire to be. In recognition of both his dedication to his sport and to his country, he was awarded both the Presidential Medal of Freedom and the Congressional Medal of Honor.

Roberto Clemente was already famous as a groundbreaking baseball player when he died in a plane crash on December 31, 1972. He was not the first Latino player in the Major Leagues, but he was the first Latino to win a World Series, an NL MVP award, and a World Series MVP award; he also received numerous Gold Gloves and All-Star selections. Clemente surely would have been elected to the Baseball Hall of Fame on the grounds of his baseball achievements alone, but his charitable work throughout Latin America earned him admiration as a humanitarian hero as well. That he died while trying to deliver aid also confers on him the especially exalted status of someone willing to sacrifice his life in the cause of helping others. Like Robinson, his hard work and discipline in the areas of both baseball and service to others enabled God to make use of him in the world beyond baseball.

More recently, Mariano Rivera has never been shy about declaring his faith in God and his gratitude for all the blessings God has showered on him throughout his life. "Mo" grew up in a fishing village in Panama; he was so poor that he and his friends had to use milk cartons for baseball gloves and tree branches for bats. From those very humble beginnings, Rivera rose to become the most revered closer in history of the game. Despite a slight physical build and no early formal coaching, he remained in the Major Leagues from 1995-2013, becoming an exemplar of achievement through hard work, consistency, discipline, and a clean life style; his "farewell tour" during the summer of 2013 made it very clear that he was being honored as much for who he was as a person as for how well he played the game. I myself heard him preach at a church near my home in upper Manhattan; he was very clear that he viewed baseball as a platform for spreading the gospel, and not as an individual pursuit for personal gain.

Of course, Rivera was compensated very well towards the end of his career, and there is absolutely nothing wrong with that. Financial rewards can and often do follow those who are faithful to God. But not always. Society does not always reward talent and faith with money. The racism and unfair labor practices that sullied the MLB from its inception mirrored those of our wider American society. But those who were faithful to God, despite challenges and even persecutions, rose to heights that even the most talented cheater could never hope to attain.

Aspire to be the best you can be – and aspire to do it the right way.  God's rewards can never be taken from you.

Robinson. Clemente. Rivera.  Some of the best players – and people – who ever played the game. None of them cheaters.  All of them men of faith.

As Jesus himself says in the gospels, "Go thou and do likewise.

# ABOUT THE AUTHOR

*Rhonda Joy Rubinson* is currently priest-in-charge of the Church of the Intercession in Manhattan. A life-long baseball fan, Rhonda was "born to the Yankees" when the obstetrician who delivered her refused to shut off the radio broadcast of the 1958 World Series while delivering her. Born of Jewish heritage, Rhonda was baptized in 1987 at the Cathedral Church of St. John the Divine, NYC, where she was one of the founding wardens of the Congregation of Saint Saviour. Since her ordination to the priesthood in the year 2000, Rhonda has also served as assistant priest at the Church of the Heavenly Rest and priest-in-charge of St. Philip's Episcopal Church in Harlem. A graduate of Barnard College, the Columbia University Graduate School of Arts and Sciences, and Union Theological Seminary, Rhonda enjoyed a long career in dance, music, and theater production prior to her ordination. A breast cancer survivor, Rhonda is also the author of *Lessons of the Spirit: A Christian Spiritual Companion for Your Breast Cancer Journey.*

www.ingramcontent.com/pod-product-compliance
Lightning Source LLC
Chambersburg PA
CBHW030154070426
42447CB00032B/1190